WALKS AROUND Pickering

10 WALKS UNDER 6 MILES

Dalesman

Dalesman Publishing Company Ltd
Stable Courtyard, Broughton Hall,
Skipton, North Yorkshire BD23 3AZ

First Edition 1999

Text © Nick Channer

Maps by Jeremy Ashcroft

Illustrations © Christine Isherwood:
p5 curlew, p9 woodmouse, p10 rabbits, p16 larch, p20 coltsfoot and
horsetails, p 23 yellowhammer in hawthorn, p28 wood anemones,
p31 goldcrest

Cover: Thornton le Dale near Pickering by Deryck Hallam

A British Library Cataloguing in Publication record
is available for this book

ISBN 1 85568 159 5

Printed by Amadeus Press, Huddersfield

Contents

Introduction

As well as being the headquarters of the North York Moors Railway, Pickering is the largest of Ryedale's four market towns and may even be the oldest, claiming to date from 270 BC. Known as the Gateway to the Moors, Pickering lies along the southern edge of the national park, making it a popular base for walking and touring.

It was during the 11th century, under William the Conqueror, that the North York Moors witnessed their bleakest period. Soon after he was crowned, the English saw fit to rebel against their new king; William quelled the rising, but in so doing destroyed vast tracts of land, burned down houses and slaughtered many people. As a precaution against further insurrection, and as a symbolic endorsement of his great power and influence, the king built many fortifications in the North of England. He certainly built a castle at Pickering but the ruins you see here today date from a later period.

The first walk in this book takes you on a magical tour of Harwood Dale Forest, just a short drive from the North Yorkshire and Cleveland Heritage Coast. With ample tree cover, this route is perfect for a warm summer's day. Nearby is the village of Burniston, only a stone's throw from Scarborough and the starting point for a gentle country walk which explores undulating moorland and farmland straddling the National Park's eastern perimeter.

Two walks begin in the centre of Pickering, while a third starts in the lowland village of Kirby Misperton, a few miles to the south. Nearly 400 acres of wooded parkland here provide the setting for Flamingo Land, a zoo and fun park inhabited by more than 1,000 birds, animals and reptiles. From the route of this walk, which runs alongside the Flamingo Land boundary, there are magnificent views north to the ridge of the moors. Neighbouring Thornton-le-Dale, one of North Yorkshire's most famous villages, is the starting point for a very pleasant, delightfully undemanding stroll across gentle farmland to the south, while further east, at Snainton, you can climb above the village into glorious parkland before heading for picturesque Wy Dale.

North-east of Snainton lies Sawdon and from here you can discover the delights of the Wykeham Forest. To the east of the forest, the final walk in the book takes you out along the banks of the 19th-century Sea Cut, returning on tracks and paths which thread their way through peaceful Raincliffe Woods — a memorable experience in any season.

Harwood Dale

Length of walk: 4 miles
**Start/finish: Harwood Dale Forest. Park in lay-by at the junction of the
A171 and the road for Staintondale and Ravenscar, north of Cloughton**
**Terrain: Woodland and field paths and tracks. Stretches of quiet road. No
steep climbs. Muddy in places**

*The heart of Harwood Dale Forest is explored on this glorious woodland walk.
There are tantalizing glimpses of the dale between the trees and a convenient inn
is located a short distance from the walk's start and finish point.*

Follow the road signposted Staintondale and Ravenscar. Look for a footpath
on the right, cross a small footbridge, skirt the field in a clockwise direction
and head down to some trees in the bottom boundary. Descend a steep
grassy bank to a footbridge and make for a stile a few strides beyond it. Turn
left, skirting the field to a footpath sign and stile up ahead in some gorse
bushes. Bear left to another stile and head across the field to the road,
keeping the tree-shaded Thorny Beck down to the left.

Turn right, pass a bungalow and bear left after about 100 yards, by a turning
on the right, to join a footpath. Cross the field, making towards a wood, and

look for a waymark in the bottom
boundary. Follow a vague path
cutting diagonally right across the
next pasture, heading for an opening
in the hedge. Cross a footbridge and
continue on the path between
bracken and trees. Turn left at the
next junction, then left again after
several yards at the second junction.

Follow the clear path and when it
becomes enclosed by trees, look for a

waymarked opening on the left. Continue on this path between trees and bracken, cross several stiles and up ahead are the rear quarters of a public house. Keep to the right of the Falcon Inn, passing through its car park to reach the road. Cross over to a field and head obliquely right to a gate leading out to the A171.

Go straight over to a stile in the grass verge, then cross the field to the far right corner. Continue ahead in the next field to a gate, cross a stony drive and take the rough track between the trees. Follow it down to a junction, go straight over and continue on a wide track for about 50 yards. Bear right to join a narrow path and follow it across a carpet of moss and lichen. Cross a forest ride and keep going, following the waymarks. Eventually the path reaches the edge of a large clearing, reminiscent of a battlefield. Turn right and follow the muddy track along the edge of this open expanse and just before a break in the trees on the right, turn sharp left and follow the outline of a track towards the left corner of a plantation.

Stay on the path as it runs along the edge of the trees, with a stone wall and field over to the left. There is a glorious view of Harwood Dale ahead. Moor Cottage Farm, the walk's next objective, can be seen nestling below the wooded escarpment. Harwood Dale offers a variety of walks, with surfaced paths designed to enable wheelchair users and the less active to enjoy an easy, gentle walk throughout the year. Some of the hay pastures in the dale are cut late to allow plants to thrive and flower. Other areas of grassland are managed to benefit a wide variety of birds – including owls, curlews and lapwings.

Make for a gate and walk alongside paddocks. Follow the fence down to the next gate and then go straight on down the tarmac farm track until you reach gates either side of it. Turn left and skirt the field, keeping fence and hedge on the left. Pass several gates and continue to a stile in the left-hand boundary. Cross over and aim diagonally right down the field slope to a second stile.

Turn left to join the road in the centre of Harwood Dale and walk up the hill out of the village. Follow the road for about half a mile, take the sharp right bend and continue for about 180 yards to reach a signposted bridleway on the left. Follow the straight track alongside the hedgerow and fence, skirting fields and rough pasture. Head for Harwood Dale Forest, passing through a gate into trees. Keep on the rough track to a junction, turn left and after a few steps, when the clear forest track curves to the right, join a parallel bridleway rising above it.

Follow the high-level, waymarked path through the woodland and bracken, with glimpses of neat, orderly rows of conifers cloaking the slopes to the left. When the path bends right, continue ahead through trees, passing through a clearing of grass, scrub and bracken. On reaching a junction, with a gate on the left, turn right and follow the track for about 70 yards. Bear left at the bridleway sign and cut through a forest break to the road. Cross the A171 by the entrance to Teydale Farm and return to the lay-by.

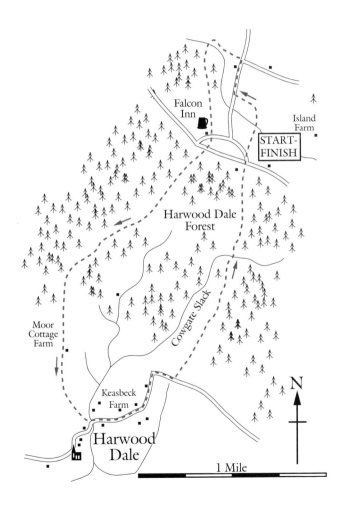

Burniston

Length of walk: 5 miles
Start/finish: Burniston village centre; the village lies at the junction of the A171 and the A165
Terrain: Paths, farm tracks and stretches of road

Overlooking the coastal plain, this memorable walk explores undulating moorland and farmland straddling the national park's eastern boundary. Beginning in the straggling village of Burniston, the path crosses field pastures to Beacon Brow and Silpho Brow, part of a line of hills representing the eastern spur of the moors.

Close to the Three Jolly Sailors pub, in the centre of Burniston, is a very useful map indicating public rights of way in the vicinity. The map is part of a new initiative, instigated by the Parish Paths Partnership, to encourage people to use the footpaths and bridleways within the parish boundaries.

Burniston, once a favourite haunt of smugglers, also marks the eastern end of the Cleveland Way Missing Link, pioneered by outdoor writers Malcolm Boyes and Hazel Chester in 1975 as a means of connecting the two ends of the long-distance route. From here the Missing Link follows a scenic route along the southern North York Moors to Helmsley, crossing the little-known Tabular Hills.

Make for the Three Jolly Sailors at the main road junction, cross over into South View and follow the lane to the edge of the village. Continue ahead in the field, keeping the hedge on the right. Look for a gate at the top of the field, turn right and pass a waymark. Follow the track as far as a dilapidated gate on the left and climb gradually through the fields. Keep going on the track as it curves left, then bears right through a gateway. Turn sharp left, then right after a few strides. Follow the track as it swings right and left before reaching the road. Cross over to a footpath sign and stile. Head diagonally across the field to the next road and turn left.

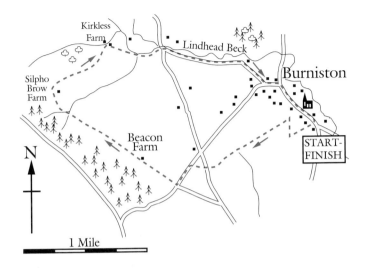

Take the first turning on the right, following the farm road towards Beacon Cottage Farm. Pass Beacon Farm further on and continue between fields, through several gates.

At length, the track runs alongside the buildings of Silpho Brow Farm. Pass the entrance to the farm, then bear right towards Kirkless Farm, following the track across the fields. Approaching the farm, veer right and head for the road. Go straight across at the junction and follow Lindhead Road back to Burniston. Turn right at the junction with the A171 and return to the centre of the village.

Dalby Forest

Length of walk: 4 miles
Start/finish: Low Dalby visitor centre car. Park off the A169 north east of Pickering
Terrain: The walk follows clear, firm tracks and forest drives from start to finish. The standard of waymarking is excellent and all the routes are consistently clear and well maintained, though conditions may vary according to the season and the weather. Long steady climb on outward leg

An easy circuit which keeps within the boundaries of Dalby Forest, an area beloved of walkers, horse riders and cyclists, as well as a vitally important habitat for wildlife. Providing fine vistas of the Dalby Forest and striking views of the valley around Low Dalby, the walk finishes by calling at the Dalby Visitor Centre, where detailed information on the forest is available.

Walk away from the visitor centre parking area, heading north along Dalby Forest Drive. Part of the North Riding Forest Park and offering a host of outdoor attractions, Dalby Forest is a hugely popular recreational resource. Pass a waymark and just beyond it is a sign for Snever Dale, Norse for narrow valley. Turn right here and take the cycle track into the trees. Pass a barrier and continue into the forest, climbing gently between bracken-covered slopes through the afforested dale.

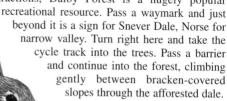

During the 18th century Dalby Forest was used as a commercial breeding ground for rabbits, with as many as 16,000 of them culled every year. Relics of the old traps and warrens can be seen in the

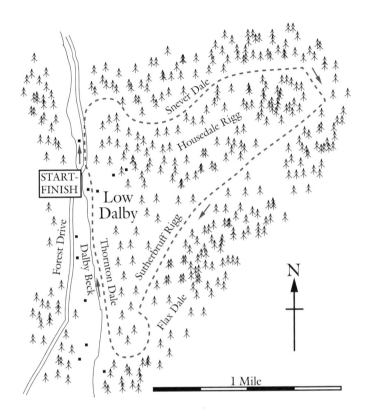

woods. The track curves gradually to the right to reach a junction of three tracks. Take the middle track and continue to climb steadily through the trees.

Turn right at the next T-junction, pass a turning on the right and cross over a forest drive. Take the next track on the right and head south-west towards Sutherbruff Rigg. Cross over a junction of tracks and cut between bracken-carpeted clearings into the trees. Pass a disused quarry on the left; piles of felled timber, stacked high in readiness for transportation to the saw mills, can often be seen on this stretch of the walk. Avoid a track running off to the right and soon bending left, and continue ahead. A track runs off sharp right and a grassy path branches off to the left at the next junction. Disregard both turnings and keep going in a south-westerly direction. Pass some mixed woodland, including beech, and follow the track sharply to the left.

Shafts of sunlight can sometimes be seen between the regulated rows of trees on the right, but such is the density and concentration that even on the sunniest day the scene amid the tangle of branches is eerily dark – like something from the pages of a children's classic fairy story. Follow the track as it curves to the right and drops down to the next corner of the woodland. There is a memorable view of the forest from here, stretching towards Thornton Dale. The track bends right again to reach a major junction. Go straight over and take either of the two right-hand tracks. They merge after about 80 yards.

Follow the main track as it bends to the right and merge with a drive at a sign for Flax Dale. Laburnum trees and wild cherry make up the scene on the right. Pass a turning for Little Dale, then a barrier and a sign for Horse Box Park and continue on the main drive. On reaching forest workers' cottages at Low Dalby, turn left, then right after a few steps by a copper beech tree. Call at the visitor centre and return to the car park.

Pickering and Beacon Hill

Length of walk: 3¹/₂ miles.
Start/finish: Beck Isle Museum, Bridge Street, Pickering. There are plenty of car parking spaces in the town.
Terrain: Stretches of road, tracks and field paths. Muddy in some places. No steep climbs.

Essentially flat and roughly rectangular-shaped walk which starts from the centre of Pickering and then heads south to Vivers Mill before returning to the town via Beacon Hill.

According to legend, Pickering was founded by Peredurus in 270 BC. The town was originally a manor of the Earls of Northumbria, and subsequently the Norman kings and the Dukes of Lancaster. Pickering's parish church of St Peter and Paul includes some remarkable 15th century wall paintings which were discovered under whitewash in 1851 by a vicar who described them as "purely ridiculous". Such was his disdain that he ordered the murals, thought to have been completed by a travelling artist, to be covered up as soon as possible. However, the paintings, which depict religious and legendary subjects, vividly recalling the lives of our saints, were eventually restored and revealed to an appreciative audience in 1879.

Begin at Beck Isle Museum in Bridge Street, a striking Regency building which houses examples of rural life in the recent past, cross the road and pass alongside the Memorial Hall. Head along Train Lane to the A170 and cross over to Vivers Lane. Follow the road until you reach a wicket gate and stile at the point where the road bends sharp right. The path runs south, keeping alongside the Pickering Beck, before passing to the right of Vivers Mill. Keep on the lane, following it round to the right to a junction at what is known as Four Lane Ends. Go straight over to join a track and stay on it to the next junction.

Turn right and follow the track through two gates, then across several fields to a gate leading to a grassy lane. Follow the lane to another gate, cut along the north side of McKechnie Vehicle Components and turn right into Westgate Carr Road. On reaching the A170, bear left and follow the opposite pavement until you reach a narrow lane which takes you to Middleton Road. Turn right and walk towards Pickering for about half a mile. Bear left on reaching Swainsea Lane and walk past St Joseph's Roman Catholic school on the left. Look for a public footpath on the right and follow it to Beacon Hill, keeping the sports hall and grounds of Lady Lumley School on the left.

From here there are very good views towards Pickering and its ruined castle. On reaching the end of a road, bear left along a path between fences, following it over two stiles and around the school sports field before dropping down the bank and turning right to a stile leading onto a wide track. Bear right and return to the centre of Pickering.

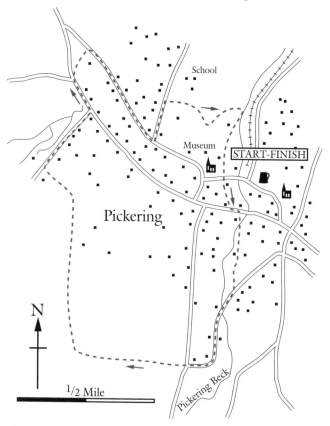

Pickering and Newbridge

Length of walk: 5 miles
Start/finish: Pickering railway station car park
Terrain: Mainly field and woodland paths. Muddy in places after rain

Starting at the North York Moors Railway headquarters, the walk skirts Pickering Woods to reach High Hunt Bridge on the Pickering Beck. From here the walk makes for the ruins of Pickering Castle.

Pickering represents the North York Moors Railway's southern terminus and it is to the old station building that thousands of people come every year, to begin an 18 mile train ride through the heart of the National Park to Grosmont near Whitby, evoking fond memories of the golden age of steam travel. The railway, including engines in steam, regularly appears on British television, most notably in the ITV drama *Heartbeat*.

It was in May 1836 that one of the wonders of the North of England was officially opened. Like all great ideas, the Whitby to Pickering railway evolved as a dream in the mind of George Stephenson, but by the 1830s the project was at last reaching fruition. Construction had begun, the dream had turned to reality. The railway's chief role was to help Whitby traders transport their goods inland, but the line also enabled passengers to travel across the moors in safety.

The line eventually closed in the 1960s, after more than 130 years in service. It lay dormant for several years while a group of dedicated enthusiasts campaigned vigorously to revive it. Their efforts eventually paid off and in 1973 the line reopened as Britain's second longest preserved railway, running steam-hauled services along one of the most scenic routes in the North of England, with miles of afforested gorges, sheltered green valleys and unprotected moorland providing a constant, unfolding backdrop.

Leave the station car park by heading towards the road. Bear left immediately before the 'stop when lights show' sign and cross the beck, turning right on the opposite bank. Cross a stile and follow the path through a meadow. Avoid the path running up the bank, keeping to the lower route as it passes to the right of some trees on the far side of the meadow. Cross a tarmac lane and follow the path between hedges. Negotiate another stile, turn right and head for the riverbank. Bear left on reaching the water and follow the path to a gate. Join a track between trees and hedges and at this point steam trains can sometimes be seen on the right, coming in and out of Pickering station. Pass a house and follow the path between banks of undergrowth.

Go through a gate and follow the track between fields to a galvanized gate. Turn immediately right to join a tarmac path, pass to the right of some houses, go through two white kissing gates either side of the railway track and cross the beck once again. On reaching the road, cross over and take the drive leading through the estate yard at Lowther House. Follow the path as it winds gently uphill along the boundary of Pickering Woods, with Pickering Beck and the line of the North York Moors Railway seen down below in the valley.

Further on, a stile leads you out into a long field; walk the length of it to reach a second stile. Once over it, follow a wide path between trees, cross a small footbridge and continue to High Hunt Bridge. Herons can often be seen on this stretch of the walk. Avoid the bridge by taking the path to the right of it, soon climbing dramatically uphill alongside a stone wall. As you approach the top of the slope look for a low wall leading to the right and head through the trees with the wall on your right. Cross a stile into a field, keep to its edge and walk alongside the woodland through several more fields. The path can then be seen cutting half left across the corner of a field to a stile. It continues through the middle of the next field before maturing into a broad track known as Love Lane. Nursery gardens make up much of the scene hereabouts.

When you reach some greenhouses, turn right to join a signposted path and follow it alongside conifer hedging and hawthorn. As you approach the steep woodland bank turn left and follow the path as it skirts the perimeter of a deep quarry. With the ruins of Pickering Castle on the left, follow the path as it heads towards the road. Just before the castle grounds, turn right and follow the path alongside a dilapidated wall. On reaching the road, cross over to the pavement and return to the railway station car park.

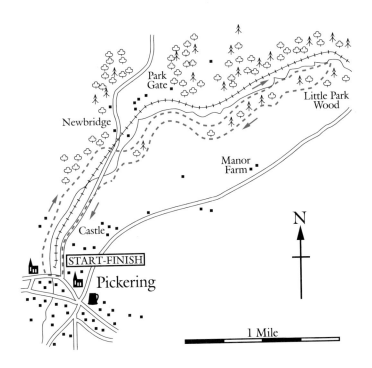

Park Gate

Little Park Wood

Newbridge

Manor Farm

N

Castle

START-FINISH

Pickering

1 Mile

Kirby Misperton

Length of walk: 2¼ miles
Start/finish: Kirby Misperton, 1½ miles west of the A169, 5 miles south of Pickering. Park at the western end of the village
Terrain: Stretch of road, farm track, field boundary paths; no hills

Level circuit with superb views stretching to the foothills of the North York Moors. The timeless, natural beauty of Yorkshire's lowland country and the man-made family attractions of Flamingo Land conspire to give this walk a unique ancient and modern theme.

The village of Kirby Misperton lies in the shadow of Flamingo Land Theme Park and Zoo, the largest privately owned zoo in the North of England. Kirby Misperton Hall and its 375 acres of wooded parkland provide a most attractive setting for one of Yorkshire's most popular family attractions. The site's tree-fringed lake is the haunt of pink flamingoes — always a popular feature with visitors. Derelict until the early 1960s, Kirby Misperton Hall dates back to the 18th century and was built for George II's illegitimate son, banished to the wilds of Yorkshire to avoid a royal scandal.

Walk away in a westerly direction, passing a cemetery and School House Court. Continue on the road to Glebe Farm and a public footpath is seen on the right just beyond it. This forms the return leg of the route, so avoid the path and stay on the road, following it as it cuts across a vast, prairie-like landscape. Extensive fields stretch like a green patchwork to the southern foot of the North York Moors.

Continue to a junction of waymarked tracks. Bear right at the sign for Great Carr Farm and follow the farm track as it snakes gently through the fertile countryside. In the distance, the ridge of the North York Moors can be seen defining the horizon. Over to the right the attractions of Flamingo Land loom into view, the roller-coaster rides and other modern mechanical structures contrasting oddly with the Yorkshire countryside. Continue along the track towards Great Carr Farm and turn right just a few yards from the farm buildings. Cross a stile and follow a waymarked path to a second stile and a galvanized gate beyond it.

Continue to the corner of the next field and cross a footbridge enclosed by two stiles. Turn right and pass lines of caravans, with the boundary hedge on the right. Pass into the next field and maintain the same direction to the field corner. Pass through the gap in the hedge and continue ahead in the next field. Swing left in the corner and make for the caravan park boundary. Cross it, turn right and follow the drive between caravans and mobile homes. When the drive bends left, veer right into the cul-de-dac and join a path heading south. There is a hedgerow on the right and a fence on the left. Follow the path all the way to the road, cross a stile, turn left and return to Kirby Misperton.

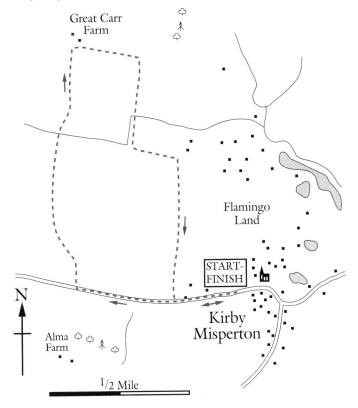

Thornton-le-Dale

Length of walk: 3¹/₂ miles
Start/finish: Main car park in the centre of Thornton-le-Dale. The village is situated on the A170, about 2 miles to the east of Pickering
Terrain: Stretches of quiet road, tracks and field paths. Low-level walking with no steep climbs

Lowland walk over farmland, with extensive views across the Vale of Pickering.

Back in the early part of the 20th century, readers of the *Yorkshire Post* voted Thornton-le-Dale the most beautiful village in Yorkshire. There may be competition from other picturesque villages in the county, but most

would surely agree that Thornton-le-Dale, which, somewhat confusingly, is often shown on maps as 'Thornton Dale', continues to retain a special place in many people's affections. Its regular appearances on calendars, postcards and biscuit-tin lids certainly confirms its enduring appeal among tourists and regular visitors.

One of the village's most famous features is the little Thornton Beck, which flows beside lines of picturesque houses and quaint cottages. Look for the little humped bridges which cross the beck, linking these village properties to the Malton road, and note also the small green in the centre of Thornton-le-Dale, where the market cross and a set of ancient village stocks

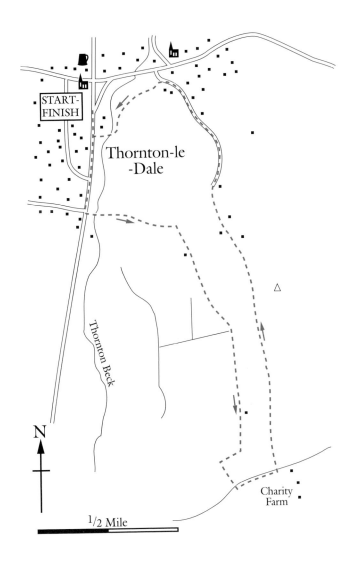

START-FINISH

Thornton-le
-Dale

Thornton Beck

N

Charity
Farm

1/2 Mile

can still be seen. Opposite are Lady Lumley's Almshouses, a row of twelve dwellings dating back to 1670 and still occupied.

The churchyard is where Matthew Grimes, a veteran of the Peninsular War, is buried. Grimes, who died in 1875 aged 96, was a soldier who helped to guard Napoleon during his exile on St Helena and was even a pall-bearer at the Emperor's funeral.

Follow the main drive from the car park down to the road and turn left, heading south out of Thornton-le-Dale. Turn left opposite Westgate and cross two footbridges by the ford. Follow the track, bearing left when you reach a double garage. The broad track cuts between trees before reaching a stile on the right. Cross over and head diagonally left across the field to a stile. Turn left for a short distance in the next field, then drift over to the fence and hedge corner. Keep the boundary on the right and make for two stiles which are reached after about 50 yards. Cross the field to another stile and continue ahead in the next pasture. Pass under the route of a dismantled railway which once linked York, Helmsley and Scarborough.

Keep the boundary on your left as you cross the field, making for a stile in the corner. Look for a waymark and follow the vague outline of the path diagonally left. Cross a little footbridge before turning right to join Harrow Cliff Lane. Follow the lane through right and left bends to a Dutch barn and hay store. Turn left and walk along the muddy track towards the buildings of Charity Farm. Avoid a footpath on the right, turning left just a few yards before it to go through double gates into a field. Follow the hedgerow, keeping it on the right, and progress along the boundary of an elongated field for some time.

Pass into the next field at a waymark and look for two circular drinking troughs for cattle either side of the gate. Continue to the top right corner of the field where there is a stile. Cross into Longlands Lane and head north. Pass a footpath on the left and, where the ground drops down gently, there are views of the early stages of the walk. Pass a green lane known as Bottons Lane on the left and follow the road as it curves gently round to the right to reach a junction.

Bear left here and follow the wide road into Thornton-le-Dale. Allotments and an adjacent cemetery can be seen on the right. Turn left opposite Rectory Lane to join a signposted footpath running through the trees. Follow the path alongside paddocks enclosed by wooden fencing and soon you reach the car park where the walk began.

Snainton and Wydale

Length of walk: 3 miles
Start/finish: Snainton, situated on the A170 midway between
Pickering and Scarborough. Space to park outside the village hall in
Barkers Lane, on the south side of the main road
Terrain: Field and parkland paths, stretches of road and track. Several
quite stiff ascents on the outward leg of the walk

Lovely walk offering a mixture of wooded parkland and open downland slopes with views stretching to the Vale of Pickering and beyond.

Snainton, nine miles west of Scarborough and bisected by the busy A170, is a long, straggling village of more than 800 residents, which won the area's 'best kept' title for two years. From Snainton you can take a scenic drive through Troutsdale to the charming village of Hackness, exploring secret valleys and undisturbed pastures along the way. The route is known as 'The Little Switzerland of the North'.

From Barkers Lane in Snainton, cross the A170 into Lairs Lane, noting the war memorial on the corner here. Pass Lairs Crescent and Rydale Rise and continue beyond the houses on a green lane running up the hillside between trees and high hedges. Look for a gate and a seat further up; don't go through the gate, but instead turn right and follow the field path. To the right is a magnificent view of the countryside to the south of Snainton, through which snakes the River Derwent.

Follow the field path all the way to

23

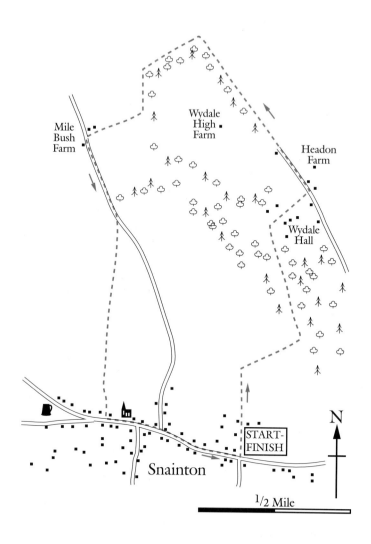

Mile
Bush
Farm

Wydale
High
Farm

Headon
Farm

Wydale
Hall

START-
FINISH

N

Snainton

1/2 Mile

a gate in the corner and at this point you are treated to a tantalizing glimpse of Wydale Hall set amidst trees and rolling parkland. Originally occupied by the Illingworth family, who owned most of the land and farms in the area, Wydale Hall is now an Emmaus Centre and a retreat for the Diocese of York. Turn left and pass a sign 'please keep dogs on lead'. Walk alongside beech trees and larch trees and when the path forks keep to the lower, more prominent route, following it down to the right of the woodland. Make for a gate and stile and cross over to a track. Turn right and walk up the estate road, passing alongside Wydale Hall. Look for a waymarked path on the right just beyond the hall and follow it alongside sturdy beech trees and within sight of greenhouses.

Go straight over at the next path junction and follow a stone wall to a kissing gate. Once through it, follow the concrete drive to a second kissing gate. Turn right to the road and then bear left. Pass Headon Farm Cottages and when the road curves left by a house, go straight on along a green lane. Go through a gate and eventually you come to a junction of tracks. Bear left and head south-west through Wy Dale. Game birds, including pheasants, can often be seen fluttering about in the vicinity of the track. Follow the bridleway and farm outbuildings can be seen diagonally across the field on the right.

Further on, the track bends left to reach a sign which denotes the high water mark of the great flood caused by the cloudburst of May 1910. A raging torrent, thirty yards wide, swept down the dale carrying all before it. Two large stone gateposts, walls and farming implements formed part of the debris.

Avoid the 'strictly private — keep out' sign and stay on the main track, following it as it rises up to the right. The bridleway runs across the fields and eventually reaches the road. Turn left and pass Granary Cottage almost immediately. Follow the road as it begins a gentle descent down into the valley. The scene here is enhanced by views across to distant hills. Pass a bridleway on the right and then swing half right by a barn to join a track known as Cliff Lane. Further on, it drops down steeply through the trees on the approach to Snainton. The sound of traffic on the A170 is audible now. On reaching the main road, turn left and walk through the village to Barkers Lane where you started.

Sawdon and the Wykeham Forest

Length of walk: 3³/₄ miles
Start/finish: Sawdon village centre, 2 miles north of Brompton on the A170 between Pickering and Scarborough
Terrain: Stretches of quiet road, field paths and woodland tracks which can be wet and slippery. Several reasonably undemanding ascents

Picturesque circular walk which starts in the village of Sawdon and soon makes for the southern fringes of Wykeham Forest. The return leg is a fine mixture of open fields and sheltered woodland.

Begin by the Anvil Inn in the centre of Sawdon and walk up the village street between stone cottages and occasional modern houses. Pass a footpath and telephone box on the right and follow the lane out of the village. The road cuts between hedgerows and wide, grassy verges. Keep going until you reach a signposted bridleway on the right. Follow the track down to Cockmoor Cottage and swing left into the field in front of it. Keep to the perimeter path, with the trees on the right. Very soon a waymark is seen. Pass through the gap in the vegetation and follow a sometimes overgrown path down into the woods. Descend beneath a canopy of trees to a junction of paths.

Turn right to reach another junction after about 50 yards. Bear sharp left and walk through this wooded valley on a damp, often muddy path. Swing sharp right very soon, curving right a little further up. Pass alongside banks of invasive bracken and keep on the clear, grassy track which soon curves left and begins a long climb through the trees, an attractive mixture of conifer and deciduous woodland. Follow the track up through the valley, all the way to a gate and stile leading out to the road.

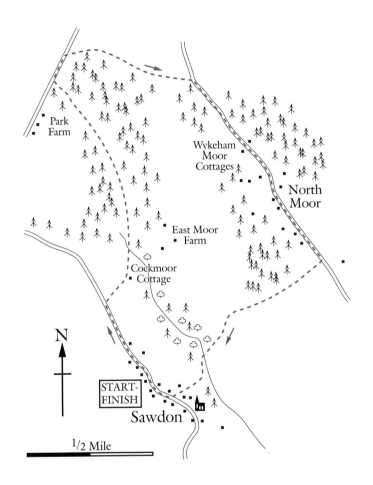

Bear right and walk along the road for a short distance, with delightful views over fields and forest. Take the first track on the right, following it as it picks its way through the trees. Keep left when the track forks at a sign for East Moor Farm and stay on the main hard track as it rises round to the right after a few yards. Follow the track along the edge of the forest and note the occasional vistas, providing teasing glimpses of the North York Moors.

Stacks of logs may well be seen along this stretch of the track, piled high in readiness for transportation to the saw mills. Turn right at the road and pass a bridleway on the right and a track on the left. Continue down the road to the buildings of Wykeham Field Station, which is used for forest research. There are some forestry houses over on the left.

Wykeham Forest extends to over 2,500 acres and includes various earthworks and other remnants of ancient history. But this corner of the North York Moors looks firmly to the future too, playing an important scientific role in assessing the health of trees, as well as monitoring their growth rate and providing seedlings to other forests.

Soon you emerge from the tree cover and there are good views now over open fields and farmland. As the road bends left, on the approach to Wykeham Grange, turn right and follow a bridleway along the field edge. There are very good views across the moors from here. Make for bridleway and footpath waymarks in the field corner and continue in the next field, following the route of the footpath. Aim for a stile on the right-hand edge of the woodland ahead. Cross into the wood and follow the path as it picks its way between rabbit holes, over a carpet of pine needles. Take the sunken path down through a rather striking gully strewn with rocks and boulders covered in moss and lichen.

Step over the Sawdon Beck, bear left, then right, then left again before following the path as it runs parallel to the beck. As you approach the Sawdon Beck again, turn sharp right just before the water's edge and follow the muddy bridleway through a gate and up the valley slope. There are splendid views of Sawdon Dale further up before an ornamental stone wall suddenly looms into view on the right. Follow the path alongside it and join a drive. After a few steps you are back in the centre of Sawdon again, opposite Glebe Farm.

Raincliffe Woods

Length of walk: 3¹/₄ miles
Start/finish: Green Gate car park, 2 miles north of East Ayton on the A170
Terrain: Stretches of road, grassy embankment, field paths and woodland tracks. One quite long steady climb

Varied walk which follows part of the Sea Cut, a hand-dug drain, before sweeping away to the south-east to enter Raincliffe Woods.

Glancing at the trees of Raincliffe Woods, it is hard to believe that this walk is so close to Scarborough. Victorian visitors to the seaside resort often made excursions to this peaceful spot. The woods, the haunt of birds such as chiffchaff and goldfinch, lie to the north-east of the Forge Valley. The steep-sided valley, through which runs the River Derwent, was cut by melting ice water towards the end of the last Ice Age and these 6,000-year-old deciduous woodlands form a link with the ancient wildwood which once covered much of England. Forge Valley takes its name from the 14th century iron forges which were fuelled by charcoal made in the surrounding woods and worked by the monks of Rievaulx Abbey. Oak trees grow on the upper slopes of the valley, while ash, elm, alder and willow are to be found on the lower flank, close to the river.

From Green Gate turn left and walk down to the junction. Bear right and follow the sign for Hackness. The road cuts between the trees, running parallel to the meandering River Derwent over on the left. Pass several modern stone bungalows and more mature dwellings on the right, and over to the left, beyond the river, are the spectacular wooded slopes of the valley.

Avoid the track to Thorn Park Farm and continue along the road, turning right immediately before the Sea Cut. This hand-dug drain, a feat of engineering by any standards, was designed and excavated by Sir George

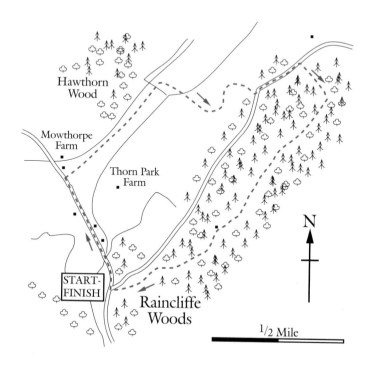

Cayley in the 19th century to divert flood water from the River Derwent to the sea at Scalby Ness, north of Scarborough. Sir George also designed a successful aircraft 50 years before the Wright brothers. The unpowered machine, a glider with a movable tailplane and undercarriage, carried his protesting coachman for 50 yards across Brompton Dale.

Follow the sign for Scalby and walk along the grassy embankment above the drain. Look back after a few moments and you gain a very pleasant view of the stone road bridge with its graceful twin arches. Cross a stile and continue along the embankment. Keep an eye out for power lines, trees and a gate on the opposite bank. About 100 yards beyond the gate, as the curtain of woodland on the far side begins to sweep away from the cut, look for a clump of bushes and some wooden steps leading down the bank to a stile. The bushes, projecting up the bank, represent the first outcrop of vegetation on this stretch of the cut.

Cross a wooden footbridge and walk diagonally across the field to a gate, heading towards the spectacular escarpment of Raincliffe Woods. Continue ahead in the next field, keeping gorse bushes on the left. Make for a gate in the field corner, avoid the track on the right and approach two gates. Pass through the gate on the left, denoted by a bridleway sign, and follow the track with a ditch on the left. Go through a gate, continue on the track and keep a tongue of woodland on the left.

As you approach the corner of the field, veer right towards a stile ahead in the trees. There is a ditch hard by you on the left and away to the east the red roofs and grey and brown stone walls of various houses and cottages can be seen amid the slopes of the valley. Once across the stile, follow the path through the trees to the road. Turn left and walk along to Raincliffe Gate. Make for the left-hand corner of the car park and follow the path up through the woodland. Further up, the path broadens out to a track, curving round to the right through the trees. It bends left, then right again and meets a path shooting in from the left. Don't turn sharp left but head through Raincliffe Woods in a south-westerly direction, keeping to the main path.

Lines of silver birch trees can be seen over to the left, on the upper slopes of the valley, while to the right the scene is dominated by coniferous woodland. Follow the track to a picnic area situated in a clearing where an assortment of tables and benches enable you to pause and enjoy a little light refreshment. A map of Raincliffe Woods helps you to work out precisely where you are and put the walk in some kind of perspective. Suitably refreshed, continue on the track past some old corrugated shacks and barns. Avoid the lower track and continue through the woodland to the car park at Green Gate. There are glorious views across the Sea Cut towards the village of Hackness as you approach the end of the walk.